Peace Maps

poems by

Karen K. Lewis

Finishing Line Press
Georgetown, Kentucky

Peace Maps

for Will, who knows that life is a river of poems

Copyright © 2020 by Karen K. Lewis
ISBN 978-1-64662-252-8 First Edition
All rights reserved under International and Pan-American Copyright Conventions. No part of this book may be reproduced in any manner whatsoever without written permission from the publisher, except in the case of brief quotations embodied in critical articles and reviews.

ACKNOWLEDGMENTS

Several poems in this collection were originally published or exhibited in different form in the following publications or venues:

"Cartography" first appeared as "Maps V (Sky);" and "Prayer Beads" first appeared as "Prayer Necklace" in *Drumvoices Revue*
"Zuma" was first exhibited as a collage "Blue Zuma" at Antioch University Los Angeles in *Know Thyself*
"Blindness and Sight" first appeared as "To See" in *Occupy SF: poems from the movement*
"Sanctuary" first appeared as "Innocents;" "Quail" first appeared in *Welcome Home*
"Dry Creek" first appeared in *Liberty Hill Poetry Review*
"Archipelago" and "End of the World Story" were first exhibited at the Artists Co-op of Mendocino in *Ekphrasis*

Publisher: Leah Maines
Editor: Christen Kincaid
Cover Art: Justin Lewis
Author Photo: Sharon Garner
Cover Design: Elizabeth Maines McCleavy

Order online: www.finishinglinepress.com
also available on amazon.com

Author inquiries and mail orders:
Finishing Line Press
P. O. Box 1626
Georgetown, Kentucky 40324
U. S. A.

Table of Contents

Cartography	1
Zuma	2
Blindness and Sight	3
Chernobyl	5
Beirut	6
Painted Cave	7
Archipelago	9
Song for a Daughter's First Birthday	10
Sappho's Island	11
Drought	13
Sanctuary	14
Summer Solstice Stargazing	15
Dry Creek	16
Sian Ka'an Biosphere	17
Small Pearls Cast of Moon Molecules and Venom	18
Tunis	19
Prayer Beads	20
Blue Dragonfly Place	23
Oaxaca	24
Chaco Canyon	25
Summer River	26
Quail	27
Desolation Wilderness	29
Place of Echoes	30
Peace Summit	32
End of the World Story	33

Cartography
[https://www.loc.gov/maps/]

Once upon a time there were no maps.
Then came dreams marked in sand, rivers, oceans
muddy sketches to warn of a snowy mountain's hidden precipice,
gold leaf to illuminate kestrel's nest, serpent's cave, pirate's lair.
Desert dwellers created an atlas of watering spots.

Armies of weary men now chart weapons
of mass destruction—false maps,
true. True maps, false. The collective moral compass
    spins wild:
        there be serpents here, mariners have always known.

Philosophers ponder boundaries to love—
Or maybe those who feel no boundaries are drawn to philosophy.
Poets are like cartographers, scribbling scratches against stone
with ink mixed of equatorial meteor minerals
risking prison, trial by fire, or disappearance—
guided by faith and galactic waypoints.

After a map has been torn
or lost   or burned   or stolen
the cartographer may pause—like a poet or a child,
listen for kestrel calls, smell turning tides,
surrender, breathe, touch ash and salt to tongue.

Then begin anew—with a blank space of possibility.
X   X   X   X   X   X   X
What spots will be marked, crossed, named, erased?
Conquered territories are perpetually revised
by armies, oracles, fires, floods,
refugees.

Once upon a time, there were no maps.
Where will our world end?
Where was the first star born?
Where does your heart touch lightning?

Zuma
[34.018, -118.833]

You are blue. Not the definition of sorrow-sad; more like the ocean on a day without fog, without cloud. You are drenched in layers of cobalt, teal, turquoise, lapis-lazuli—this limitless amnion churning between air and fire. Colder depths pull swirls of current around your torso, while the deep-dark claims your eyes and tints them indigo. You meet each wave where turbulence pounds your faith into thin kelp ropes entangling your waist. You claim the water's gift of infinity. You are not aware that seawater anoints the smallest molecules within. During a blind, breathless instant, opal sparks your unborn son's heart. Salt tints your future daughter's eyes with sapphire. You do not know how long the swell will hold, or whether the next wave brings a ride or a wipeout. You simply plunge into each wave and claim effervescent shards of a perpetually shattered aquamarine mirror.

Blindness and Sight
[9.859, 105.982]

An eye for an eye makes the whole world blind.
~Mohandas Gandhi (attributed)

      A leg for a leg
Son for son
      Daughter after daughter,
trauma follows trauma
      we fall into delirious
misery of unmarked graves.

No shoulders
      No hands
Elbow for elbow,
      Heart for a heart
beat by beat. Let us
      tear unborn twins from a mother's womb
to keep things s y m-

m e t r i ca l.

Ear for an ear—
we are trapped now in silence,
      thick like a lead coffin.

We listen for seven billion
      pairs of footsteps that march
detached
      from their platoons of legs

toward an abyss without angels.

Wing for wing
      Feather for feather
Knife against knife
      Bullet for bullet
Fist to fist

Let us occupy this space

between clouds

pulled by capricious gravity
invisible and urgent like

    memory.

        It has been told
        that blind warriors
        (and children) can
        read
        with their finger-
        tips—

        F i n g e r s
            c l i m b
        b r a i l l e

            m o u n t a i n s,

then
crumple
ancient parchment scrolls
    light them to fire,
        light many fires.

Smoke spirals to
sting grieving eyes with napalm rain

    while Earth awakens
        every new day at dawn.

Billions upon billions of eyes
pulse and glimmer on
fear-drenched seas
    refugees drowning
between tides of
    revenge.

Chernobyl
[51.388, 30.097]

I searched for red, and
did not notice it in the morning bird's whistle
or during a flash of opalescent
stars spiraling along our galaxy's farthest curve.
No trace remains of crimson in the forest
        only ivory blossoms, ebony bark, the viridian
of frog songs around a toxic pond,
the pond's moss surrounding frogs.

        Across the Baltic
        silence.
        Across the Mediterranean:
        silence.
        Across Arctic ice:
        silence.

Traces of wolf skin and butterfly wings coalesce
        in amber swollen on tainted cherry branches.
On another continent, pyres drift down ashy rivers
        adorned with incense and gold-bordered shrouds.
Burnt sienna crumbles from ancient chapel ceilings
        while my prayers bow to dusk.
Cyclical winds scatter invisible particles—
        molecules to nourish my quickening son.

        Everywhere on Earth: silence.

Beirut
[33.880, 35.442]

Words on walls. Messages from seekers.
Yearning for the missing.
During a lull in the bombardment, artists
stencil colorful designs on new ruins.
Their paint is ground from helixes
of old angers   and seashells.
Nobody will issue graffiti citations.

Cradled within rubble—chips of glyphs, cuneiform, the glitter
of extinct civilizations—torn languages and bent chrome,
how to write this sound? A heartbeat between moon and sea.

Love dances with confusion and love's disguises.
Another building destroyed. A child is born, delivered by faith.

A white stork stands, resting at low tide, free to remain, free to fly
beyond where things that should not burn, are burning.
Dark eyes seek silence, summon a scattered flock,
wings are building strength for tomorrow's onward migration.

Painted Cave
[34.504, -119.787]

After he has gone to work,
morning breeze brings traces of old fires,
while I lullaby our infant to nap and worry
    about smog from Los Angeles staining the horizon
        beyond the Channel Islands

    where families once gathered—then scattered.

On the path to our house, built
    in wildfire-charred Chumash territory,

        I walk barefoot on sandstone
        and crushed acorns, yet cannot
        remember the trail song of my grandmothers.

        People
still catch dreams, decipher cosmic symbols,
        nurture children.

    Complex emotions
are now expressed as digital symbols
        manipulated by fingertips and machines
            bursting as invisible pulses through cyberspace.

There is an hour for sun to ripen sage,
        an hour to seek fish and feather,
            an hour to shelter in caves,
to paint designs with charcoal and blood, oxide and bone.

I hold this infant's heartbeat,
an owl's echo,
        oak branches rustled by wind
    waves of ocean against
        broken shells.

A man went to war, returned,
    built a fence of century plants and boulders,
        built a home,
birthed a son,
    sought redemption,
        went off to work at the Islands again today.

    I will
      splash
           sweet creek water

onto our son's feet, his face
his newborn fists.

      May he build peace.

Archipelago
[-16.802, 179.519]

A hidden atoll, barely ten paces wide at high tide, sometimes resembles a postcard paradise. Other times only a celadon mirage, glittering with remains of broken shells and hatchling turtle tracks. Hours earlier (escaping a bitter quarrel) she'd plunged, unobserved, into the lagoon's temporary refuge. Now she tastes salt and blood on her coral-scraped wrist. She stretches out on rough sand, in slim shade of a coconut palm. Scientists say that coral polyps will take root and colonize human skin. She imagines remaining on the islet forever, allowing high tide to wash over, day by day, month by month, until the pearl within quickens, breathes, cries. Or until coral claims her skeleton. Mermaids are born from broken hearts—they battle pirates and sharks, navigate loss—guided only by faith and declining moonlight.

Song for a Daughter's First Birthday
[44.807, -124.069]

    A glimpse of
           old gates left swinging open—
                a missing
        hour of almost-afternoon.

Oak leaves lift with breeze-tangled ribbons
stellar song   wind rush   fog silence.

Dusty summer-grass days spiral
        with narrow fern-green glimmer moments—all stolen
            by that trickster
                who hides inside ocean's sorrow-shadows.

Cradle her,
newborn daughter-gift,
effervescent, heart-brave, anointed by a
        salt-damp touch of butterfly wings
            floating with last-light's flight.

Sip steamy tea brewed
    from smoke-scented dream petals
        stirred by splintered star-space of a father's absence.

        Let moon-fire
        pour iridescent glimmer-guides
        to light her daughter-journey in all directions.

Sappho's Island
[39.276, 26.356]

Poetry lingers in graffiti—torn ciphers, fragments

of what happened, or what might happen,

or what might never happen

or secret

[   ]

    Poetry relies on space

    between breath

    between words

    between letters

      [   ] bodies that [   ]

    between splashes of ink

    on [   ]

    Poetry relies on resonance

        between

    waves of love, or hate, or apathy, or prayer

Poems are gestures of true-moments, courage

of a poet who signs her name with indelible ink

    beneath words

      [   ]

    upon [   ] between

beloved soldiers and [   ] refugees
When emptiness cannot be deciphered
    after ink has faded
    papyrus burned
    translations twisted
    walls bombed to rubble
    cave carvings eroded
    after graffiti has been dissolved
    over   and over   and over
        with bitter tea and blood and flame
Fragments of poems remain, like tourniquets
    to mend our fatal hemorrhage
        of despair

Drought
[-21.792, 31.776]

The Shona mother is wrapped in a shawl
of yesterday's hunger and hope
her skirts whisper like dry river sand rippled by wind

    she follows an elephant trail, seeking water.

    Her people burned forest
    to plant fields of maize—
    and no rain came
    this year, or last.

Her child grew without adequate milk
without siblings, his
eyes deeper than mud ponds
where women once gathered to dance and flirt.

    The young mother wears
    a necklace of gold and charm stones
    for protection
    but her jewels are a heavy burden,
     scratching thin skin,
    her every breath a bargain with unseen gods.

Someone else's children wail. A cheetah hides in the shade.

    The river sings no song except emptiness
    in this season of no dancing.

Finally—here,
among scattered river rocks and mopane roots

    a place that might yield water
    if she can dig deep enough into sand—
    if her plastic water-carrier will endure
    the long journey home to the village.

Sanctuary
[hidden]

Tonight
they are safe and snug
beneath ribbons and red flannel
hiding from winter fog.
    Our fire ripples warmth.
    Sketchbooks and homework papers
    camera, stuffed bear, toys, kittens
        are scattered
    in a chaotic and innocent utopia.

Wondering days of simple moments
when our children play
with rubber balls and mud paint
and their skin is stained
with berry juice,
injuries mended
with sticky cartoon bandages.

In tonight's cocoon of dreams,
I know where our children rest, for they are here.
Rain taps primitive rhythms on our rooftop
    and we have a rooftop
    and we are together
    and we have eaten dinner.
    No malevolent soldiers
    pound the door,
    nor mortar our yard
    and we have said grace.

Summer Solstice Stargazing
[39.303, -123.795]

Night summons us to an abyss of rhymed imagination
where instinct knots blue helixes to find imagination.

I dream about the taste of summer's moon and salty stars
curled within courage of my daughter's kind imagination.

What song do migrating whales whisper? Ancient trees
scatter sparks across damp sand, while oracles rewind imagination.

Galactic prayers summon children born of love, not
violence—along unexplored latitudes of blind imagination.

Indigo nights delight the poet and her daughter,
who listen for bronze chimes of infinite imagination.

Dry Creek
[38.705, -123.081]

In the forest of manzanita and madrone
branches whisper
as fish thrash upstream
against the pulse of gravity.

Spawn will die in
autumn's dry arroyo but
the salmon swim anyway
following a spiral code
to toyon-banked streams where
ancestor flesh once sang in the fire.
Ashes swirl like quail feathers
that once flew,
now caught in tree moss.
Flesh now ashes, minerals bled to the stream
where sisal grass grows elbow tall
where baskets once were
woven
once were broken.

Wind whispers
crawling like a caterpillar
through oak leaves
calling cloud
weaving cloud
swimming cloud
pounding mortar and pestle until
rain falls
in roe-sized drops no longer red
but clear,
clear as crystals, each drop reflecting
silence.

Sian Ka'an Biosphere
[19.942, -87.465]

We are walking on a beach littered knee-deep in trash.
This is a biosphere preserve with promises of shells, not trash.

Plastic of every color and shape, blue lids from *Agua Crystal*
High tide delivers bountiful tons of barnacle-encrusted trash.

While coconut palms grow ever taller, sweet with flower
Morning brings sea grass and skeletons of birds tangled with trash.

On a beach so remote that few humans step ashore, the power
of industrialized civilization scatters its message-laden trash.

Behold the jagged edge of a colonized continent, ultimately
abandoned to sea turtles, fishermen, mosquitoes, and trash.

Planeta Azul, Crystal, Colgate, Clairol, Coppertone Sport,
Too many castaway green *Inca Oil* bottles from Venezuela—trash.

The *Coppertone* is from Memphis, and promises "*No CFC's*".
Infinite shards of plastic will poison creatures not evolved to eat trash.

Mangroves provide sanctuary for Italian shampoo, *Brisa, Kraft.*
Nestlé Dominica. Coca Cola. Countless plastic combs: trashed.

Random solitary shoes: flip-flops, heels, *Nike, Adidas*. Each a refugee.
Hopeful beachcombers will create new art from trash.

But every tide brings more debris: a red lid claiming positive energy,
Heineken's green star, doll parts. *Rubbermaid. Pepsi. Noxema.* Trash.

Small Pearls Cast of Moon Molecules and Venom
[37.433, -122.176]

Your tissue is sliced and cells stained in a laboratory hundreds of miles from home and you are trapped in a long, long moment of waiting, similar to being at the chaparral trail's edge next to a rattlesnake that you almost stepped on, but didn't. Now you are staring cancer in the face. It may have already sunk its venomous mutations into the molecular geometry of your body. The snake went her way and you continued up the mountain. The view and breath from each step of the trail felt sacred. Another day. The doctor does not call. You remember being trapped in a wave off Byron Bay, how the riptide sucked you under and panic stung like jellyfish. When the swell lifted you, freed you—you swam for shore cradled in the purest amnion. Then—wipeout. You held your breath, sand crushing skin. You thought oh, this is how swimmers die. Prisms of light swirled through your fear. Now, somewhere in the city a scientist—like an oracle—gazes into their crystalline lens, seeking the truth of your future, scratching symbols onto paper, like a fortune.

Tunis
[36.795, 10.002]
from a news photograph

Your veil conceals
thin scars, labor's rust, tribal designs that mark a woman
like my grandmother once pierced my ears, gave me her earrings,
taught me to endure pain that every woman holds.

Excitement blooms from your eyes
like tulips, topaz, fire sparking a quest for freedom.

Echoes of gunfire, the third call
to prayer chanted from mosaic minaret, jets scream
across an impossibly lapis-blue sky.
Your eyes sting from tear gas and rage and hope.

Smoke and secrets,
the taste of sweet mint tea,
your sister's blood on your fingertips—
she is still smiling, calling into the crowd
wounded, struggling to stand.

Whispers of ash, the zoom and click
of a camera's limited focus.
Another mourning ceremony will soon begin.

Later, you and your sister will restore your veils,
walk hand-in-hand through
jasmine-scented stone passageways,
her arm bruised and bleeding
beneath silver bracelets, your shoes broken.

You will find new routes to the heart of your labyrinth
As I seek mine, a continent apart.

Prayer Beads
[33.264, 44.383]

☉

There is no blue swimming pool in Baghdad,
only the muddy pulse
of ancient rivers.

☉

Nobody wants to swim there anymore.
Anymore, anymore.
Children are still laughing in the ruined gardens.

☉

Pleasure is warped, like the mahogany skin
of a boat trapped in sand, or like a bird's wing
stripped to the bone.

☉

Stains: rust, charcoal, calligrapher's ink.
Do not forget blood.
Pomegranate. Memory.

☉

The weapons truck grinds its steel gears
uphill, crushing one silver necklace
of prayer song.

☉

It's really all about fire.
Sparks. Fire.
Flame.

☉

Waiting for rain.
Rain. Rain.
Silence.

☉

When fire enters wood
a louder breath escapes—
molecules of heart.

☉

Shattered porcelain. Abandoned marble.
Bronze ears tarnished by salt
beneath an inland sea.

☉

Your daughters scream from the volcano's heart.
A branch snags the soft belly of a wildcat
who will devour your sons.

☉

Do you mourn your lost twin's cry?
The touch of his skin?
The echo of footsteps?

☉

Twelve beads.
One prayer:
Love.

Blue Dragonfly Place
[39.275, -123.789]

Empty canyon, hidden stream
Only quail calls and silence.

    Then the voice of wind
    Awakening trees.

        Alder leaves are falling, where
        Spider webs trap sunlight.

Oaxaca
[15.667, -96.571]

Four pelicans translate ocean and sky
Eyes skim aquatic reflections of time
Tilt wings, then plunge, trap fish, and fly

Lost whales migrate, like deep memories rise—
Shadows anchored to earth, all hearts pump brine
Four pelicans translate ocean and sky

I wonder if pelicans hear me cry—
With hearts built of cloud, our spirits align
Raise wings, then plunge, catch fish, and fly

Humans build temples to desire's cry,
hollow silences, bones shredded by time—
Four pelicans translate ocean and sky

Steel jets scratch war through dawn's blue dye—
Pelicans choreograph tidal wave-rhyme,
Lift wings, then plunge, claim fish, and fly

Noon's bell rings while turtle skulls hide—
Sun climbs, whales breach, tide turns, shadows decline
Four pelicans translate ocean and sky
Raise wings, then plunge, claim fish, then fly.

Chaco Canyon
[36.063, -107.964]

The question of mesquite,
near water, not far from fire
and howling coyotes—a thirst
twisting deeper than roots between
boulders.

The question of rock,
where gray and blue sky
whirl across circles of stones
shaped twice: by earth, by hands—
once settled, now abandoned.

A question of the lost egg
from that rust-stained bird
whose shadow stalks us—
wings, feathers, empty sky,
thorns.

A question of snow
sudden, falling in silence
to cover our
footprints.

Summer River
[39.179, -123.701]

Yellow blossoms cover traces of ash and agate along the trail where he leads us to a secret swimming place. One daughter sings in the language of osprey and the other whispers to a brown turtle the size of her fist. The turtle crawls across our path and disappears into its ancestral stream. Our shadows crisscross each other. A solitary gray osprey soars to a branch-built nest on top of a lightning-snagged fir. Both daughters splash into the river shallows pursued by salamander bubble-songs. My husband plunges after (to keep them safe) while I dream this poem from yellow blossoms and barefoot summer mud.

Quail
[blurred]

The children and I ride a moment of laughter
and delirium of a summer day.
We were playing at the beach,
now dusk summons us home.

The whoosh of our car flushes a covey of quail—
they fly at low altitude across the paved road.
Elders flank at least twenty fledglings.
    Thud.   Thud.

The children stop laughing.
I stop the car. Climb down.
Cradle one quail chick in the palm of my hand
Feathers warm as summer grass, neck limp,

Quail's spirit a rough regret released
from my hands to the sky.
Fledgling quail know little, yet
of roads, cars, people.

The second small body trembles.
Looking at me. Looking at me.
I lift the chick, place it near the dead one,
berry thorns scrape my wrist,
another smear of blood.

Parent quail concealed in roadside bramble thickets
Make click-throated calls
Scolding her scattered chicks. Scolding me.
Summoning the covey home. Warning me away.

The children are full of questions I cannot answer.
We leave prayers on the road, windblown feathers.

I'm crying but must carry on, there is no choice
we are in the middle of the road
my mind spinning—this sharp shame.

I double-check the children's seatbelts.
We are nearly home.

Desolation Wilderness
[38.875, -120.082]

We woke up next to the lake
startled by the sounds of trout splashing
Wisps of fog swirled with frog shadows
Our breath mingled with mist
Juniper branches and memories scented our fire
Yesterday, two flocks of geese flew northward
After midnight, scattered coyotes sang to the stars
This morning, I am unsure whether to follow the
trout, the coyotes, or the geese
Maybe I will linger here in the shade, with you
I am like a juniper with branches twisted
in ten thousand directions—
touching clouds.

Place of Echoes
[14.835, -89.148]

Stone has
  collapsed
    into
      sacred
chaos.

Each bears the weight of moss
  and questions wedged
    between gravity's demands
and river-flood.

Butterfly wings—torn and
fossilized to rust rock
scattered everywhere.

Lightning paints obsidian feathers,
  wind scatters macaw song and corn seed
    in this canyon of prayers—
unanswered.

We linger in shadows where owls hunt at dawn
  Scarlet birds whistle.
    Whistle bird,
whistle our hearts open to a hidden path.

River-dark eyes follow traces of old scribes
  whose glyphs disappear
beneath moss and mud.

Lost emperors and goddesses rest
  surrounded by volcanic serpents—coiled, engraved,
    indifferent to our shallow
footprints and breath.

Tomorrow we will climb
   to the summit,
      said to be crowned with hollow bones
  of those who knew how to fly.

If we find quills, we will dip them
          in dream-blood mixed with rain.

Peace Summit
[27.984, 86.915]

one wind	one song
many silences	many languages
one star	one sky
many planets	many desires
one summit	one fire
many routes	many embers
one raindrop	one vision
many thirsts	many eyes
one seed	one love
much hunger	many hearts

End of the World Story
[39.142, -123.735]

We woke at first light. The waning moon glowed with salt mist. Wind pulsed through pine trees while a seed cone fell onto muddy ash. The ocean endured, rolling and rolling onto shore. Pelicans glided along eternal sorrow-trails while we searched for lost friends. A shrine to fallen warriors had collapsed. Each lichen-encrusted granite and marble boulder lay scattered and crushed by waves of turning tide. Gulls danced and picked through kelp and debris arriving from distant continents. We could not hear whistling swans wing north that day. Stellar sea lions and elephant seals guarded their secret sea caves. High tide buried our footprints with radioactive glitter-sand. I wanted to believe in a driftwood raft where children would sing and splash in morning sun, anointed by pure water and prayers. If this were the last story at the end of the world, it would be scribed with bone in sand, or blood on stone, charcoal on skin, or dream on star-constellated sky. The ultimate word would be silent, invisible: *love*.

Karen K. Lewis lives in rural Northern California between the forest and the sea, on unceded ancestral land of the Pomo people. She holds an MFA from Antioch Los Angeles. She attended Mount Holyoke College and earned a BA from Stanford. Once upon a time, Karen lived and traveled widely overseas. She and her husband, the sculptor Will Lewis, co-parented four children who are now grown. Karen's fiction, essays, and articles appear in anthologies and journals including *Iron Horse, Literary Mama, Weave, Instant City, Minerva Rising, Teachers and Writers,* and *Hip Mama*. Karen is a former Director of the Mendocino Coast Writers' Conference and leads workshops with California Poets in the Schools. She is a seven-time recipient of California Arts Council—Artists in Schools grants. She's also passionate about farm-to-table cooking, foraging, and conservation of ecosystems (including removal of ocean plastics). She believes in the healing power of words.

www.ingramcontent.com/pod-product-compliance
Lightning Source LLC
LaVergne TN
LVHW041603070426
835507LV00011B/1272